ॐ

CHANDI HOMA DEVI STUTI

Essence and Sanskrit Grammar

Ya Devi Sarva Bhuteshu

Ashwini Kumar Aggarwal

जय गुरुदेव

ISBN13: 978-93-95766-51-7 Paperback Edition
ISBN13: 978-93-95766-49-4 Hardbound Edition
ISBN13: 978-93-95766-50-0 Digital Edition

Title: **Chandi Homa Devi Stuti**
SubTitle: **Essence and Sanskrit Grammar**
Author: **Ashwini Kumar Aggarwal**

Printed and Published by
Devotees of Sri Sri Ravi Shankar Ashram
34 Sunny Enclave, Devigarh Road,
Patiala 147001, Punjab, India

https://advaita56.in/
The Art of Living Centre

https://www.artofliving.org/

25th March 2023, Durga Homa at Bundela Mandir Patiala with offering of Sari, & nav Kanya & Gau puja. Chaitra Navratri Shukla paksha, Vinayaka Chaturthi, Lakshmi Pancami. Bharani upari Krittika Nakshatra.

Vikram Samvat 2080 Pingala Saka Era 1945 Shobhakrit

1st Edition March 2023

जय गुरुदेव

Dedication

Sri Sri Ravi Shankar

who taught us Mother divine worship, Old Meditation Hall below Sumeru Mantap, Navratri Oct 2003, Bangalore Ashram

Acknowledgements

Chandi Homa with Guru Puja, Devi Abhisheka and Havan reciting verses from Durga Saptashati, Satsang and Aarti at Bundela Mandir Patiala 5:00pm to 8:00pm, 25th Mar 2023, followed by nav Kanya Puja & Gau Puja. On the occasion of Chaitra Navratri.

Front Cover Photo Courtesy

A painting at The Oberoi, Marine Drive, Bombay. Photo by Ashwini dated 1st March 2023.

Blessing

Two things make you dance in your life:
One is your desire, another is love.

There is a dance that comes out joy, that comes out of love. That deep love makes you dance. In this dance, you do not get tired. Shraddha grows when a desire is fulfilled but when one desire does not get fulfilled the faith gets shaken. In love you don't get shaken. You shake the whole world. Not just the world, but the entire universe. You make the angels and the Gods dance.

Sri Sri Ravi Shankar

Photo courtesy Guru Puja Havan 10 March 2014 Patiala

Preface

Etymology and Essence

What is Puja?
Panini Dhatupatha Root 1642 पूज पूजायाम् । to worship.
पूजा = पूर्णात् जायते इति पूजा = that which is born of fullness is called Puja.
Fullness = a state of being satiated. A state of feeling wonderful within. Being grateful.

Who is Durga?
दुर्गा = upasarga दुर् very difficult/impossible + Root 982 गमॢ गतौ 1cP । to go. to transcend.

दुर्गा = who cannot be transcended, who cannot be overcome in battle.

दुर्गा = who clears away all obstacles, who vanquishes all misery and restores bliss & prosperity.

This book presents the **Devi Stuti verses,** also known as **Tantokta Devi Sukta;** from the **5th chapter** of the **Durga Saptashati.**

Contents

Idol courtesy Navratri Puja 7 Oct to 14 Oct 2021 Patiala

सर्व मङ्गल माङ्गल्ये शिवे सर्वार्थ साधिके ।
शरण्ये त्र्यम्बके गौरि नारायणि नमोऽस्तु ते ॥

Prayer

नमो देव्यै महादेव्यै शिवायै सततं नमः ।
नमः प्रकृत्यै भद्रायै नियताः प्रणताः स्म ताम् ॥ १
रौद्रायै नमो नित्यायै गौर्यै धात्र्यै नमो नमः ।
ज्योत्स्नायै चेन्दुरूपिण्यै सुखायै सततं नमः ॥ २
कल्याण्यै प्रणतां वृद्ध्यै सिद्ध्यै कुर्मो नमो नमः ।
नैर्ऋत्यै भूभृतां लक्ष्म्यै शर्वाण्यै ते नमो नमः ॥ ३

1. Greetings to the Feminine force. Salutations to the Female form. Offerings to the Consort of Lord Shiva. Respects to the mighty primal Empress. Compliments to the Queenly power and the Shakti so evident in creation.

2. I bow down to SHE
-who makes me melt and dissolve
-who is ever present at my side
-who is so fair and beautiful
-who nourishes me thoroughly
-who is brilliant like the sun
-who is pleasant and calming like the full moon
-who is the sweet nectar in my life

3. I humbly bow down to HER
-who is behind every victory
-who inspires all growth
-who bestows all talent
-who makes even demons dance
-who makes even presidents look for external support
-who powers the good and noble and enlightens them

Idol courtesy Lakshmi Puja on Diwali 14 Niv 2020 Patiala

दुर्गायै दुर्गपारायै सारायै सर्वकारिण्यै ।
ख्यात्यै तथैव कृष्णायै धूम्रायै सततं नमः ॥ ४
अतिसौम्यातिरौद्रायै नतास्तस्यै नमो नमः ।
नमो जगत्प्रतिष्ठायै देव्यै कृत्यै नमो नमः ॥ ५

4. I surrender to that BEAUTY
-who creates challenges & hints how to overcome all
-who is my essence and my aim as well
-who engineers all events & manifests all phenomena
-who is the most famous heroine
-whose attraction sways all and draws them to her
-who shimmers like smoke and is hence uncatchable

5. I submit to the GODDESS
-who is an epitome of peace, tranquility, safety, trust
-who is fierce and brooks no offence
-who comes immediately to the aid of her kith and kin
-who is the bedrock of this universe
-who is the divine glow in all
-who is the prime mover, cause and doer of everything

Photo courtesy Ram Navmi Puja 25 March 2018 Patiala

Guru Parampara

सदाशिवसमारम्भां शङ्कराचार्यमध्यमाम् ।
अस्मद् श्रीगुरुपर्यन्तां वन्दे गुरुपरम्पराम् ॥

sadāśivasamārambhāṃ śaṅkarācāryamadhyamām I
asmad śrīguruparyantāṃ vande guruparamparām II

सदाशिवसमारम्भाम् शङ्कराचार्यमध्यमाम् ।
अस्मत् श्रीगुरुपर्यन्ताम् वन्दे गुरुपरम्पराम् ॥

सदा-शिव-सम्-आरम्भाम् $^{f2/1}$ that tradition which has perfectlyEvolved from the eternalLordShiva शङ्कराचार्य-मध्यमाम् $^{f2/1}$ the tradition that has Adi Shankaracharya somewhere in between । अस्मत् $^{mfn5/3}$ from our श्री-गुरु-पर्यन्ताम् $^{m6/3}$ extending till our current exalted Master वन्दे $^{लट् i/1}$ I salute गुरु-परम्पराम् $^{m6/3}$ tradition of sacred Masters ॥

वन्दे from Dhatupatha 11. वन्द् अभिवादनस्तुत्योः । 1cA

Painting courtesy TOK Punjab Nov 2010 Ludhiana

Devi Stuti

There is an ancient text in the Vedic tradition that goes by the name of **Markandeya Purana**. It gives various rituals and customs for family and society to observe and follow, to lead a happy and successful life. These customs are based on observing the life of real people, how they faced difficulties and overcame challenges and vagaries. Written by sage Markandeya (of **Maha Mrityunjaya Mantra** fame) it consists of 137 chapters.

Its thirteen chapters from 81 to 93 consisting of 700 verses are called Devi Mahatmya, also as Chandi Path, which is today famous as the **Durga Saptashati**.

The Durga Saptashati is recited and read in many Indian homes. Many ashrams and gurukuls organise big festivals prior to Dussehra during the autumn Navratri to commemorate this text in the form of Chanting, Puja, Homa and Celebration.

Within the Durga Saptashati, there are some verses known as the Devi Stuti or the **Tantrokta Devi Sukta**. Today it has become a custom to sing the Devi Stuti in a prayerful and soulful manner, that spreads cheer and brings great good fortune to the participants.

This book is an attempt to elucidate the deep secrets enshrined in these verses, so that the English medium school children can benefit, thereby this knowledge can spread far and wide and reach every home.

Photo courtesy 1st Dussehra 1980 Mali Ganj, Ludhiana

Eighteen Attributes of Mother Divine

या देवी सर्वभूतेषु विष्णुमायेति शब्दिता ।
नमस्तस्यै नमस्तस्यै नमस्तस्यै नमो नमः ॥ ६
yā devī sarvabhūteṣu viṣṇumāyeti śabditā ।
namastasyai namastasyai namastasyai namo namaḥ ॥ 6

या देवी सर्व-भूतेषु विष्णु-माया इति शब्दिता ।
नमः तस्यै नमः तस्यै नमः तस्यै नमः नमः ॥
या[f1/1] that देवी [f1/1] goddess सर्व-भूतेषु [n7/3] residing in all-beings विष्णु-माया [f1/1] is Lord's expressive energy इति [0] thus शब्दिता [adj PPP f1/1] it is so proclaimed । नमः [n2/1] offer bowing down तस्यै [f4/1] to thee नमः [n2/1] salute तस्यै [f4/1] her नमः [n2/1] greet तस्यै [f4/1] her नमः [n2/1] as an act of humble obeisance नमः [n2/1] felicitation to her ॥

नमः from नमस्[n] । तस्यै from तद् [mfn]

1. Māyā

That sound vibration frequency (*shabdita*) which is the bedrock of body anatomy (*bhuteshu*), expresses itself clearly (*vishnu*) in humans.

O ye notice this current, feel this energy, become aware of that intrinsic movement that never stops, that hums all the time till the end of this body.

The illustrious Goddess is called Maya, since:

- She captivates all beings, wise or powerful
- She is the wisdom that delivers liberation
- She is the illusion that keeps clever men bound
- And frees the child-like innocent pure at heart

- She manifests from the collective will
- Of all luminous stars and divine beings
- And hence she has at her command
- All the skills and strategies and weapons
- That the creation is capable of

- Thus she can attract and subdue
- Thus she is praised and glorified
- And her sparks manifest all the feminine forms
- Beautiful maidens that roam the galaxies
- Lovely women that grace every society

या देवी सर्वभूतेषु चेतनेत्यभिधीयते ।
नमस्तस्यै नमस्तस्यै नमस्तस्यै नमो नमः ॥ ७
yā devī sarvabhūteṣu cetanetyabhidhīyate ।
namastasyai namastasyai namastasyai namo namaḥ ॥ 7

या देवी सर्व-भूतेषु चेतना इति अभिधीयते ।
नमः तस्यै नमः तस्यै नमः तस्यै नमः नमः ॥
या $^{f1/1}$ that देवी $^{f1/1}$ goddess सर्व-भूतेषु $^{n7/3}$ residing in all-beings चेतना $^{f1/1}$ consciousness इति ^{0} thus अभि-धीयते $^{लट्iii/1}$ closely-she supports । नमः $^{n2/1}$ offer bowing down तस्यै $^{f4/1}$ to thee नमः $^{n2/1}$ salute तस्यै $^{f4/1}$ her नमः $^{n2/1}$ greet तस्यै $^{f4/1}$ her नमः $^{n2/1}$ as an act of humble obeisance नमः $^{n2/1}$ felicitation to she ॥

अभिधीयते = upasarga अभि + धीयते । Root 1136 धीङ् आधारे आदाने अनादरे च । 4cA = to preserve, support, hold
upasarga अभि = closely, tightly, intrinsically, fully

2. Chetnā

Commonly termed as conscious, alive and expressive, this inner energy is what makes a body interact with the external.

The other living bodies and the ever-present forces of nature can only transact, nay want-to-transact with something that is 'conscious'.

या देवी सर्वभूतेषु बुद्धिरूपेण संस्थिता ।
नमस्तस्यै नमस्तस्यै नमस्तस्यै नमो नमः ॥ ८

yā devī sarvabhūteṣu buddhirūpeṇa saṃsthitā ।
namastasyai namastasyai namastasyai namo namaḥ ॥ 8

या देवी सर्व-भूतेषु बुद्धि-रूपेण संस्थिता ।
नमः तस्यै नमः तस्यै नमः तस्यै नमः नमः ॥

या$^{f1/1}$ that देवी$^{f1/1}$ goddess सर्व-भूतेषु$^{n7/3}$ residing in all-beings बुद्धि-रूपेण$^{n3/1}$ as intelligence संस्थिता$^{PPP\ f1/1}$ is stationed । नमः$^{n2/1}$ offer bowing down तस्यै$^{f4/1}$ to thee नमः$^{n2/1}$ salute तस्यै$^{f4/1}$ her नमः$^{n2/1}$ greet तस्यै$^{f4/1}$ her नमः$^{n2/1}$ as an act of humble obeisance नमः$^{n2/1}$ felicitation to she ॥

3. Buddhi

O Man! Know that mere interaction is not desirable, albeit it is so commonplace as to be non-existent.

What is needed is the proper, smart, and constructive use of the Intellect.

Each body has been endowed with a reason. The capacity to use that reason with a broad vision, stepping out of personal and private needs and comforts, is highly desirable, and it is respected in the world of men.

Idol courtesy Bhagwat Saptah Dec 2022, Shuka Tirth Gaudiya Math, Shukratal, UP

या देवी सर्वभूतेषु निद्रारूपेण संस्थिता ।
नमस्तस्यै नमस्तस्यै नमस्तस्यै नमो नमः ॥ ९
yā devī sarvabhūteṣu nidrārūpeṇa saṃsthitā ।
namastasyai namastasyai namastasyai namo namaḥ ॥ 9

या देवी सर्व-भूतेषु निद्रा-रूपेण संस्थिता ।
नमः तस्यै नमः तस्यै नमः तस्यै नमः नमः ॥
या$^{f1/1}$ that देवी $^{f1/1}$ goddess सर्व-भूतेषु $^{n7/3}$ residing in all-beings निद्रा-रूपेण $^{n3/1}$ as sleep संस्थिता $^{PPP\ f1/1}$ functions । नमः $^{n2/1}$ offer bowing down तस्यै $^{f4/1}$ to thee नमः $^{n2/1}$ salute तस्यै $^{f4/1}$ her नमः $^{n2/1}$ greet तस्यै $^{f4/1}$ her नमः $^{n2/1}$ as an act of humble obeisance नमः $^{n2/1}$ felicitation to she ॥

4. Nidrā

And O Human! Know that just as underuse of faculties is undesirable, overuse or abuse is also to be shunned at all costs, hence welcome the desire to sleep.

Welcome the desire to drop and let go.
Welcome the moment when you are so tired that you just want to shut out everything and just be.

Welcome the disconnection from it all.

Idol courtesy Festival 13 Oct 2018 Shivananda Ashram, Rishikesh

या देवी सर्वभूतेषु क्षुधारूपेण संस्थिता ।
नमस्तस्यै नमस्तस्यै नमस्तस्यै नमो नमः ॥ १०

yā devī sarvabhūteṣu kṣudhārūpeṇa saṃsthitā ।
namastasyai namastasyai namastasyai namo namaḥ ॥
10 ॥

या देवी सर्व-भूतेषु क्षुधा-रूपेण संस्थिता ।
नमः तस्यै नमः तस्यै नमः तस्यै नमः नमः ॥

या[f1/1] that देवी [f1/1] goddess सर्व-भूतेषु [n7/3] residing in all-beings क्षुधा-रूपेण [n3/1] as hunger संस्थिता [PPP f1/1] appears । नमः [n2/1] offer bowing down तस्यै [f4/1] to thee नमः [n2/1] salute तस्यै [f4/1] her नमः [n2/1] greet तस्यै [f4/1] her नमः [n2/1] as an act of humble obeisance नमः [n2/1] felicitation to she ॥

5. Kshudhā

A part of this inner force is known as smallness, weakness, timidity. It expresses as hunger, as need for nourishment, as some oil is needed from time to time to keep a lamp lit.

Hunger makes one vulnerable. Hunger is no respecter of economic status, personal wealth, fame, power or anything else. When you feel hungry, in that moment you become weak in front of other humans, weak in front of nature. Then you must halt other activities and attend to it first.

You must satisfy your hunger first and then proceed.

Else this famish if not attended to in time, shall rob you of your immunity and make the body weak in the long run, and the price you pay later (just to appear rich and glamorous in front of someone now), shall be untenable.

या देवी सर्वभूतेषुच्छायारूपेण संस्थिता ।
नमस्तस्यै नमस्तस्यै नमस्तस्यै नमो नमः ॥ ११
yā devī sarvabhūteṣu chāyārūpeṇa saṃsthitā ।
namastasyai namastasyai namastasyai namo namaḥ ॥
11 ॥

या देवी सर्व-भूतेषु छाया-रूपेण संस्थिता ।
नमः तस्यै नमः तस्यै नमः तस्यै नमः नमः ॥
या$^{f1/1}$ that देवी $^{f1/1}$ goddess सर्व-भूतेषु $^{n7/3}$ residing in all-beings छाया-रूपेण $^{n3/1}$ as shade संस्थिता $^{PPP\ f1/1}$ protects । नमः $^{n2/1}$ offer bowing down तस्यै $^{f4/1}$ to thee नमः $^{n2/1}$ salute तस्यै $^{f4/1}$ her नमः $^{n2/1}$ greet तस्यै $^{f4/1}$ her नमः $^{n2/1}$ as an act of humble obeisance नमः $^{n2/1}$ felicitation to she ॥

6. Chhāyā

O Man! Know that just as sunlight or illumination is needed for the body to function, at the same time shade or coolness is needed for the mind to make correct decisions.

Hence

- Ensure that your workplace is well-lit and cool
- Ensure that your bedroom has soft-lighting and coolness
- Ensure that your diner has warm-glow and you eat in a shady spot.

In our Vedas, **Shade** is the wife of the **Sun**, worthy of equal honor and respect.

Opposite values are Complementary in Nature, know ye as the first maxim.

Painting courtesy AMC Dec 2010, TOK Ludhiana

या देवी सर्वभूतेषु शक्तिरूपेण संस्थिता ।
नमस्तस्यै नमस्तस्यै नमस्तस्यै नमो नमः ॥ १२

yā devī sarvabhūteṣu śaktirūpeṇa saṃsthitā ।
namastasyai namastasyai namastasyai namo namaḥ ॥
12 ॥

या देवी सर्व-भूतेषु शक्ति-रूपेण संस्थिता ।
नमः तस्यै नमः तस्यै नमः तस्यै नमः नमः ॥

या$^{f1/1}$ that देवी$^{f1/1}$ goddess सर्व-भूतेषु$^{n7/3}$ residing in all-beings शक्ति-रूपेण$^{n3/1}$ as strength energy stamina संस्थिता$^{PPP\ f1/1}$ expresses । नमः$^{n2/1}$ offer bowing down तस्यै$^{f4/1}$ to thee नमः$^{n2/1}$ salute तस्यै$^{f4/1}$ her नमः$^{n2/1}$ greet तस्यै$^{f4/1}$ her नमः$^{n2/1}$ as an act of humble obeisance नमः$^{n2/1}$ felicitation to she ॥

7. Shakti

All of you are endowed with power, strength, force, and a unique talent.

All men, whether african, indian, american, aboriginal, japanese, russian, european, chinese, or others, are endowed with **Superhuman** Strength.

Use your strength wisely.
Use your powers with discretion.
Use your talents for common and long term good.

Havan courtesy Navratri 17 Oct 2007, Vasad Ashram

या देवी सर्वभूतेषु तृष्णारूपेण संस्थिता ।
नमस्तस्यै नमस्तस्यै नमस्तस्यै नमो नमः ॥ १३

yā devī sarvabhūteṣu tṛṣṇārūpeṇa saṃsthitā ।
namastasyai namastasyai namastasyai namo namaḥ ॥
13 ॥

या देवी सर्व-भूतेषु तृष्णा-रूपेण संस्थिता ।
नमः तस्यै नमः तस्यै नमः तस्यै नमः नमः ॥

या[f1/1] that देवी [f1/1] goddess सर्व-भूतेषु [n7/3] residing in all-beings तृष्णा-रूपेण [n3/1] in the form of strong desire or craving संस्थिता [PPP f1/1] expresses । नमः [n2/1] offer bowing down तस्यै [f4/1] to thee नमः [n2/1] salute तस्यै [f4/1] her नमः [n2/1] greet तस्यै [f4/1] her नमः [n2/1] as an act of humble obeisance नमः [n2/1] felicitation to she ॥

8. Trishnā

And apart from strength, you all have an insatiable appetite, infinite ambition, unending demands.

These have been provided to you for a purpose.

Ascertain your life's aim, then quickly get set on your track. Determine your priority and align with it losing no time.

Ensure you get the right education, ensure you choose your desirable idol, ensure you select a **Guru** to hasten the process.

Remember your demands are not easy to fulfill, your ambitions cannot be quickly achieved. So, make your focus precise, make your efforts sincere, and get on the road towards the fulfilment of your goal.

या देवी सर्वभूतेषु क्षान्तिरूपेण संस्थिता ।
नमस्तस्यै नमस्तस्यै नमस्तस्यै नमो नमः ॥ १४

yā devī sarvabhūteṣu kṣāntirūpeṇa saṃsthitā ।
namastasyai namastasyai namastasyai namo namaḥ ॥ 14 ॥

या देवी सर्व-भूतेषु क्षान्ति-रूपेण संस्थिता ।
नमः तस्यै नमः तस्यै नमः तस्यै नमः नमः ॥

या[f1/1] that देवी [f1/1] goddess सर्व-भूतेषु [n7/3] residing in all-beings क्षान्ति-रूपेण [n3/1] in the form of patience and forbearance संस्थिता [PPP f1/1] manifests । नमः [n2/1] offer bowing down तस्यै [f4/1] to thee नमः [n2/1] salute तस्यै [f4/1] her नमः [n2/1] greet तस्यै [f4/1] her नमः [n2/1] as an act of humble obeisance नमः [n2/1] felicitation to she ॥

9. Kshānti

Aims need sincere efforts, aims needs patience forbearance forgiveness.

An extra mile when you are *seemingly* fatigued, beaten, lost...is usually needed to achieve the pinnacle.

For that
a sober patient forgiving attitude
becomes the deciding factor.

Nourish this trait,
become more enduring with time,
nay become as big as time itself.

Photo courtesy Saraswati Puja April 2016, AVG, Nagpur

या देवी सर्वभूतेषु जातिरूपेण संस्थिता ।
नमस्तस्यै नमस्तस्यै नमस्तस्यै नमो नमः ॥ १५

yā devī sarvabhūteṣu jātirūpeṇa saṃsthitā ।
namastasyai namastasyai namastasyai namo namaḥ ॥
15 ॥

या देवी सर्व-भूतेषु जाति-रूपेण संस्थिता ।
नमः तस्यै नमः तस्यै नमः तस्यै नमः नमः ॥

या$^{f1/1}$ that देवी$^{f1/1}$ goddess सर्व-भूतेषु$^{n7/3}$ residing in all-beings जाति-रूपेण$^{n3/1}$ by form appearance genus संस्थिता$^{PPP\ f1/1}$ appears । नमः$^{n2/1}$ offer bowing down तस्यै$^{f4/1}$ to thee नमः$^{n2/1}$ salute तस्यै$^{f4/1}$ her नमः$^{n2/1}$ greet तस्यै$^{f4/1}$ her नमः$^{n2/1}$ as an act of humble obeisance नमः$^{n2/1}$ felicitation to she ॥

10. Jāti

My friend you are born in a species, your anatomy fits some genus.

Check if you are a warrior at heart or an administrator. Ascertain if you are a sportsman or a glamor goddess.

Know your limits and limitations,
know your talents and resources.
Then live a perfect life.

Live with the knowledge that whatever your profession or vocation or occupation, you are No. 1.

You are **Ultimate** in the eyes of the Lord.

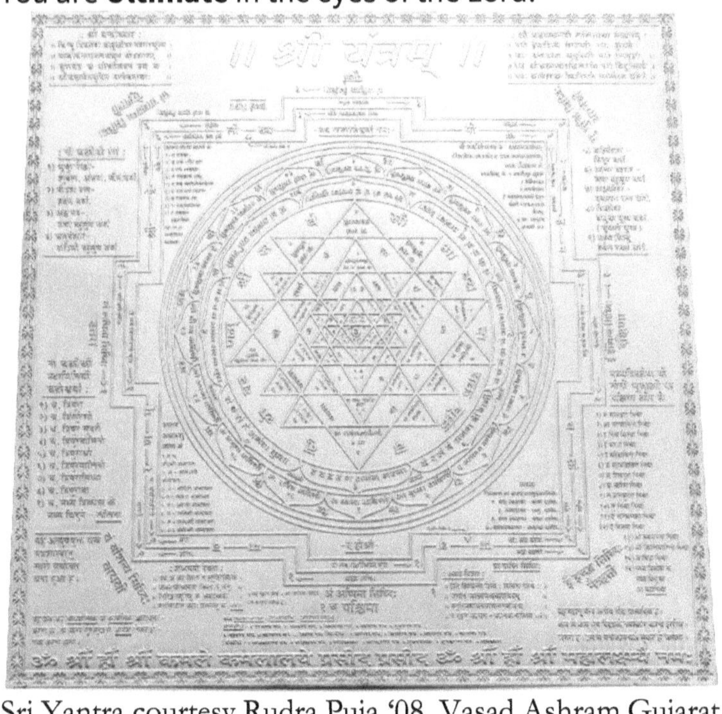

Sri Yantra courtesy Rudra Puja '08, Vasad Ashram,Gujarat

या देवी सर्वभूतेषु लज्जारूपेण संस्थिता ।
नमस्तस्यै नमस्तस्यै नमस्तस्यै नमो नमः ॥ १६

yā devī sarvabhūteṣu lajjārūpeṇa saṃsthitā ।
namastasyai namastasyai namastasyai namo namaḥ ॥
16 ॥

या देवी सर्व-भूतेषु लज्जा-रूपेण संस्थिता ।
नमः तस्यै नमः तस्यै नमः तस्यै नमः नमः ॥
या$^{f1/1}$ that देवी $^{f1/1}$ goddess सर्व-भूतेषु $^{n7/3}$ residing in all-beings लज्जा-रूपेण $^{n3/1}$ as shyness or shame संस्थिता $^{PPP\ f1/1}$ manifests । नमः $^{n2/1}$ offer bowing down तस्यै $^{f4/1}$ to thee नमः $^{n2/1}$ salute तस्यै $^{f4/1}$ her नमः $^{n2/1}$ greet तस्यै $^{f4/1}$ her नमः $^{n2/1}$ as an act of humble obeisance नमः $^{n2/1}$ felicitation to she ॥

11. Lajjā

Shyness Softness Timidity is your innate nature.

Becoming *ashamed* on making a mistake,
Surrendering unhesitatingly to the Guru,
these are aspects which make you beautiful.

These are the traits which are coveted highly by the Lord. This is the reason the Divine loves you so much, that is why a mother loves her son no end.

या देवी सर्वभूतेषु शान्तिरूपेण संस्थिता ।
नमस्तस्यै नमस्तस्यै नमस्तस्यै नमो नमः ॥ १७

yā devī sarvabhūteṣu śāntirūpeṇa saṃsthitā ।
namastasyai namastasyai namastasyai namo namaḥ ॥
17 ॥

या देवी सर्व-भूतेषु शान्ति-रूपेण संस्थिता ।
नमः तस्यै नमः तस्यै नमः तस्यै नमः नमः ॥

या $^{f1/1}$ that देवी $^{f1/1}$ goddess सर्व-भूतेषु $^{n7/3}$ residing in all-beings शान्ति-रूपेण $^{n3/1}$ as peace or calmness संस्थिता $^{PPP\ f1/1}$ is fixed । नमः $^{n2/1}$ offer bowing down तस्यै $^{f4/1}$ to thee नमः $^{n2/1}$ salute तस्यै $^{f4/1}$ her नमः $^{n2/1}$ greet तस्यै $^{f4/1}$ her नमः $^{n2/1}$ as an act of humble obeisance नमः $^{n2/1}$ felicitation to she ॥

12. Shānti

Calmness Tranquility Equanimity. Peace is a foremost quality, being peaceful in trying circumstances is what sets you apart and makes you the unquestionable leader.

Peace is not inner, hidden or covered.
Rather it is radiant, expressive, out in the open.

It makes sense to maintain calmness especially when the situation is highly volatile, when there is a serious disturbance within the family or at office, or a storm is raging outside and it shall pass on its own.

For this **Meditation** is essential, there can be no peace in the heart without a daily meditative practice.

या देवी सर्वभूतेषु श्रद्धारूपेण संस्थिता ।
नमस्तस्यै नमस्तस्यै नमस्तस्यै नमो नमः ॥ १८

yā devī sarvabhūteṣu śraddhārūpeṇa saṃsthitā ।
namastasyai namastasyai namastasyai namo namaḥ ॥
18 ॥

या देवी सर्व-भूतेषु श्रद्धा-रूपेण संस्थिता ।
नमः तस्यै नमः तस्यै नमः तस्यै नमः नमः ॥

या[f1/1] that देवी [f1/1] goddess सर्व-भूतेषु [n7/3] residing in all-beings श्रद्धा-रूपेण [n3/1] as faith or belief संस्थिता [PPP f1/1] is stable । नमः [n2/1] offer bowing down तस्यै [f4/1] to thee नमः [n2/1] salute तस्यै [f4/1] her नमः [n2/1] greet तस्यै [f4/1] her नमः [n2/1] as an act of humble obeisance नमः [n2/1] felicitation to she ॥

13. Shraddhā

Faith. Trust. Unshakeable Belief. One cannot take a single step in this world without faith.

But faith must be nurtured and ingrained for many many years to become rock-steady and unshakeable.

Only a trust that weathers the storm is of any use. Only a strong belief in your spouse or girlfriend or lover can turn the tide in your favor.

Only faith in the master comes to your rescue in trying circumstances.

Faith is the oil that keeps the joints mobile, faith is the grease that keeps the machinery moving.

Faith is the **strongest** pillar in life.

Rangoli courtesy Guruji's birthplace house, 24 May 2015
Papanasam, Tamil Nadu

या देवी सर्वभूतेषु कान्तिरूपेण संस्थिता ।
नमस्तस्यै नमस्तस्यै नमस्तस्यै नमो नमः ॥ १९

yā devī sarvabhūteṣu kāntirūpeṇa saṃsthitā ।
namastasyai namastasyai namastasyai namo namaḥ ॥ 19 ॥

या देवी सर्व-भूतेषु कान्ति-रूपेण संस्थिता ।
नमः तस्यै नमः तस्यै नमः तस्यै नमः नमः ॥

या$^{f1/1}$ that देवी$^{f1/1}$ goddess सर्व-भूतेषु$^{n7/3}$ residing in all-beings कान्ति-रूपेण$^{n3/1}$ as charm or comeliness संस्थिता$^{PPP\ f1/1}$ is available । नमः$^{n2/1}$ offer bowing down तस्यै$^{f4/1}$ to thee नमः$^{n2/1}$ salute तस्यै$^{f4/1}$ her नमः$^{n2/1}$ greet तस्यै$^{f4/1}$ her नमः$^{n2/1}$ as an act of humble obeisance नमः$^{n2/1}$ felicitation to she ॥

14. Kānti

Desire. Wish. Fancy. Fantasy. Longing. How can the world function without desire? Charm Grace Comeliness Desirable Loveliness.

What need of God or Guru if there is no charming desire. What use is Love if there is no desirable lover.

Without the beloved, all aims are insipid, without passion there can be no dispassion, nay even compassion melts in the face of passion, in the intensity of love, in the fires of desire.

या देवी सर्वभूतेषु लक्ष्मीरूपेण संस्थिता ।
नमस्तस्यै नमस्तस्यै नमस्तस्यै नमो नमः ॥ २०

yā devī sarvabhūteṣu lakṣmīrūpeṇa saṃsthitā ।
namastasyai namastasyai namastasyai namo namaḥ ॥ 20 ॥

या देवी सर्व-भूतेषु लक्ष्मी-रूपेण संस्थिता ।
नमः तस्यै नमः तस्यै नमः तस्यै नमः नमः ॥

या[f1/1] that देवी [f1/1] goddess सर्व-भूतेषु [n7/3] residing in all-beings लक्ष्मी-रूपेण [n3/1] in the form of wealth and resources संस्थिता [PPP f1/1] is present । नमः [n2/1] offer bowing down तस्यै [f4/1] to thee नमः [n2/1] salute तस्यै [f4/1] her नमः [n2/1] greet तस्यै [f4/1] her नमः [n2/1] as an act of humble obeisance नमः [n2/1] felicitation to she ॥

15. Lakshmī

Wealth. Abundance. Liquid Cash. Resources and Assets. Time a Plenty.

My dear each and everyone of you are blessed with an Abundance of Everything. God is there at your beck and call. Nature responds swiftly to satisfy and fulfill.

Discover this, invent it, and know that you are the richest man on earth, know that the entire wealth of this magnificent creation belongs to you.

Know that all beings are ready to serve you willingly when your heart is happy.

या देवी सर्वभूतेषु वृत्तिरूपेण संस्थिता ।
नमस्तस्यै नमस्तस्यै नमस्तस्यै नमो नमः ॥ २१

yā devī sarvabhūteṣu vṛttirūpeṇa saṃsthitā ।
namastasyai namastasyai namastasyai namo namaḥ ॥
21 ॥

या देवी सर्व-भूतेषु वृत्ति-रूपेण संस्थिता ।
नमः तस्यै नमः तस्यै नमः तस्यै नमः नमः ॥

या[f1/1] that देवी [f1/1] goddess सर्व-भूतेषु [n7/3] residing in all-beings वृत्ति-रूपेण [n3/1] as a stream of thoughts and modulations संस्थिता [PPP f1/1] popping up । नमः [n2/1] offer bowing down तस्यै [f4/1] to thee नमः [n2/1] salute तस्यै [f4/1] her नमः [n2/1] greet तस्यै [f4/1] her नमः [n2/1] as an act of humble obeisance नमः [n2/1] felicitation to she ॥

16. Vritti

Thoughts. Unending stream of mind arrows and beams. Only some of us are able to sit for Meditation.

And in meditation what do we sense? That our mind is an unending streak of impulses. So many memories surface, so many past situations and happenings make themselves heard. Plans anxieties and what about the future, such forebodings and misgivings keep sprouting.

My dear, it is the desire to live, to be known, to be appreciated and attended to, to make a mark and ripple in society that keeps the mind in an unending tizzy.

The one who is lucky latches on to a particular impulse and goes forward in life. He earns name, fame, wealth or power, and that is what our planet is all about.

Nothing more, nothing less.

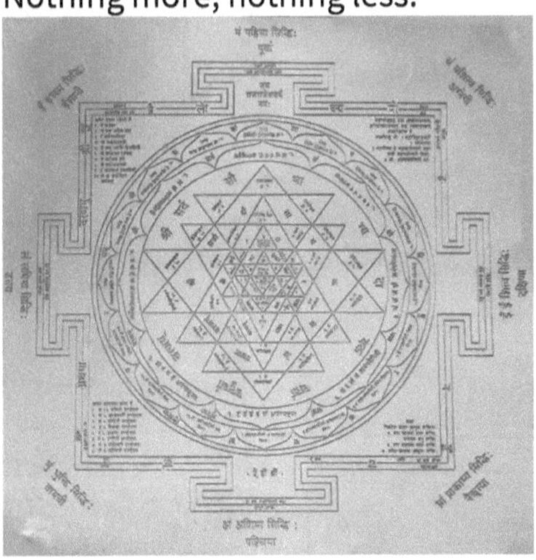

या देवी सर्वभूतेषु स्मृतिरूपेण संस्थिता ।
नमस्तस्यै नमस्तस्यै नमस्तस्यै नमो नमः ॥ २२
yā devī sarvabhūteṣu smṛtirūpeṇa saṃsthitā ।
namastasyai namastasyai namastasyai namo namaḥ ॥ 22 ॥

या देवी सर्वभूतेषु स्मृति-रूपेण संस्थिता ।
नमः तस्यै नमः तस्यै नमः तस्यै नमः नमः ॥
या $^{f1/1}$ that देवी $^{f1/1}$ goddess सर्व-भूतेषु $^{n7/3}$ residing in all-beings स्मृति-रूपेण $^{n3/1}$ as memory and impression संस्थिता $^{PPP\ f1/1}$ is stored । नमः $^{n2/1}$ offer bowing down तस्यै $^{f4/1}$ to thee नमः $^{n2/1}$ salute तस्यै $^{f4/1}$ her नमः $^{n2/1}$ greet तस्यै $^{f4/1}$ her नमः $^{n2/1}$ as an act of humble obeisance नमः $^{n2/1}$ felicitation to she ॥

17. Smriti

Memory. Flashback. Citta. The summum bonum of what a body or being or soul consists of is called Smriti or Citta.

Because of it, learning happens, growth happens, evolution happens.

Because of it a baby turns into a boy, a boy into man. Because of it companies, organizations, schools and nations function.

Because of this faculty, we are able to engineer, discover, invent and grow big.

या देवी सर्वभूतेषु दयारूपेण संस्थिता ।
नमस्तस्यै नमस्तस्यै नमस्तस्यै नमो नमः ॥ २३
yā devī sarvabhūteṣu dayārūpeṇa saṃsthitā ।
namastasyai namastasyai namastasyai namo namaḥ ॥
23

या देवी सर्वभूतेषु दया-रूपेण संस्थिता ।
नमः तस्यै नमः तस्यै नमः तस्यै नमः नमः ॥
या[f1/1] that देवी [f1/1] goddess सर्व-भूतेषु [n7/3] residing in all-beings दया-रूपेण [n3/1] as compassion and kindness संस्थिता [PPP f1/1] is expressed । नमः [n2/1] offer bowing down तस्यै [f4/1] to thee नमः [n2/1] salute तस्यै [f4/1] her नमः [n2/1] greet तस्यै [f4/1] her नमः [n2/1] as an act of humble obeisance नमः [n2/1] felicitation to she ॥

18. Dayā

Compassion. Kindness. Softness. The cornerstone of society, togetherness, family life and friendship.

There are innumerable occasions when each one of us is kind and understanding, when we go out of the way to help someone with no thought of return.

Society and Neighborhoods are filled with kindness, each mother has loads of it, the special man who achieves sainthood is because of this supreme quality that he polished well for a long time.

Compassion is not only in mothers and saints, nay every business is built on the foundation of helpfulness.

Planet Earth is what it is:
a living beautiful graceful creative and open-ended ecosystem because of its inherent kindness towards all beings and things.

Aarti - Lamps

या देवी सर्वभूतेषु तुष्टिरूपेण संस्थिता ।

नमस्तस्यै नमस्तस्यै नमस्तस्यै नमो नमः ॥ २४

yā devī sarvabhūteṣu tuṣṭirūpeṇa saṃsthitā ।

namastasyai namastasyai namastasyai namo namaḥ ॥24

a. Tushti

Contentment. Fullness. Satiated. Satisfied. Brimming with Abundance. Being supremely Grateful. A remarkable quality. A rare quality. A hidden and unexpressed emotion. A virtue that is so deep inside that it gets missed, it goes unnoticed, and is scarcely evident in the common man. Though it is all around us in nature. Plants flowers trees, birds animals bees, all exhibit it to a high degree.

The forces of creation cannot function without gratefulness, the man who becomes big always offers the credit to his parents and to God. He feels soaked in this emotion, he becomes numb by the presence of *tushti* in his life, a vibrant fullness.

या देवी सर्वभूतेषु मातृरूपेण संस्थिता ।
नमस्तस्यै नमस्तस्यै नमस्तस्यै नमो नमः ॥ २५

yā devī sarvabhūteṣu mātṛrūpeṇa saṃsthitā ।
namastasyai namastasyai namastasyai namo namaḥ ॥25

b. Mātri

Motherhood. Becoming a mom, wanting to give, wanting to share.
And what happens to someone who feels full and satisfied and grateful? He then wants to give and give and give. He wants to sing the glories of the Lord, he wants to heap praises on this creation, he wants to make another like him, he gives birth to a son.

Motherhood is the first principle of creation. From it all stems, because of it the universe expands, due to it we have babies, plants have saplings, cows have calves, and there is togetherness, belongingness, happiness, mischief and laughter all around.

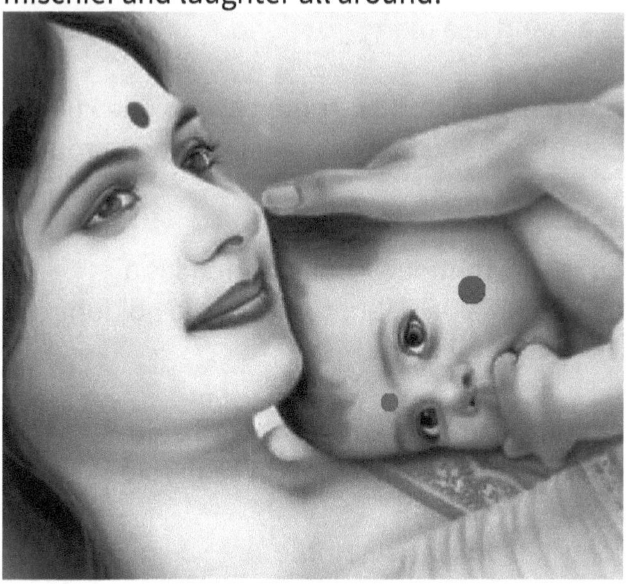

या देवी सर्वभूतेषु भ्रान्तिरूपेण संस्थिता ।
नमस्तस्यै नमस्तस्यै नमस्तस्यै नमो नमः ॥ २६

yā devī sarvabhūteṣu bhrāntirūpeṇa saṃsthitā ।
namastasyai namastasyai namastasyai namo namaḥ ॥26

c. Bhrānti

Maya. Illusion. Imagination. Projection. Leela. Sport. Just a Game.

Finally, we remember - O Ho! Aho! I am just dreaming. I am enjoying a day dream and having many dreams at night.

No need to get so tight or suffocated. No need to worry about anything. No need to feel miserable or guilty or poor or ashamed.

This is all simply magic. It is a blockbuster movie. Some have plum roles; many have sublime roles. And it all goes around in a merry go round.

Today i am rich and famous. Tomorrow no one knows me, nay i work as somebody's maid in some forgotten place.

Today i am hand-to-mouth, but my friend is a Billionaire or a President, but tomorrow is not long in coming...

Tides change, fortunes change, the Lord enjoys diversity in everything, and revels in each role.

Jai Gurudev 2:39pm Patiala Home.

Gratefulness – Flowers Fruits Sweets

इन्द्रियाणामधिष्ठात्री भूतानां चाखिलेषु या ।
भूतेषु सततं तस्यै व्याप्तिदेव्यै नमो नमः ॥ २७

i.

It is just now revealed to me. The supreme secret. The Lord dwells in my heart. He controls my senses. He germinates my desires.

The Divine **alone** rules me, and lives and expresses through me.

चितिरूपेण या कृत्स्नमेतद् व्याप्य स्थिता जगत् ।
नमस्तस्यै नमस्तस्यै नमस्तस्यै नमो नमः ॥ २८

ii.

It is now crystal clear.

How come i got born?

How come i had parents to care for me? How come i had siblings and toys and tasty things to eat and new places to visit?

How is it possible that i have a home and i have a profession and i have a place in society?

I realize just now it is all the Lord's **doing**. It is his handiwork. I feel so sublime and soaked in the Divine.

I feel so much grace and blessing pouring.

स्तुता सुरैः पूर्वमभीष्टसंश्रयात् तथा सुरेन्द्रेण दिनेषु सेविता ।
करोतु सा नः शुभहेतुरीश्वरी शुभानि भद्राण्यभिहन्तु चापदः ॥ २९

iii.

O Lord! Please forgive me. I used to be jealous of the wise, of the rich, of the powerful. I had made my own set of right-and-wrong and i had fitted you within my tiny frame.

Now i see those who are better than me or seemingly more advanced, they have more of your grace and more of your support. Surely, they must have pleased you more than i have. Now i also wish to please you, serve you, and obtain your favor.

I also wish to go ahead without being envious, without blaming or cursing anyone. Without announcing anyone as the offender, without doing any back-biting, nor any emotional blackmail.

I see the Math clearly. The threads of my thoughts have become untangled and i feel free of foolish notions and accusing temptations. I rejoice in the Supreme Knowledge that it is **you**, all is you, and i am also **yourself**.

या साम्प्रतं चोद्धतदैत्यतापितैर-स्माभिरीशा च सुरैर्नमस्यते ।
या च स्मृता तत्क्षणमेव हन्ति नः सर्वापदो भक्तिविनम्रमूर्तिभिः ॥ ३०

iv.

I rejoice in the state of *sat-chit-anand*,
a joyous conscious truth.

I now see with open eyes and a happy heart.
I now listen with glee.

Thank You. Thank You. Thank You.

Bhajan – Singing

दुर्गे दुर्गे दुर्गे जय जय मा, दुर्गे दुर्गे दुर्गे जय जय मा
देवि दुर्गे जय जय मा, देवि दुर्गे जय जय मा

काली कपालिनि मा, जगतोधरिनि मा
काली कपालिनि मा, जगतोधरिनि मा
देवि जय जय जय जय मा, देवि जय जय जय जय मा

दुर्गे दुर्गे, दुर्गे जय जय मा
दुर्गे दुर्गे, दुर्गे जय जय मा

आनन्द रूपिनि मा, करुना सागरि मा
आनन्द रूपिनि मा, करुना सागरि मा
देवि जय जय जय जय मा, देवि जय जय जय जय मा

दुर्गे दुर्गे, दुर्गे जय जय मा, दुर्गे दुर्गे, दुर्गे जय जय मा
देवि दुर्गे दुर्गे, दुर्गे जय जय मा, देवि दुर्गे दुर्गे, दुर्गे जय जय मा

देवि दुर्गे जय जय मा
देवि दुर्गे जय जय मा
देवि दुर्गे जय जय मा
देवि दुर्गे जय जय मा
https://www.youtube.com/watch?v=Q-568j_CAoQ

Durge Durge, Durge Jaya Jaya Maa
Durge Durge, Durge Jaya Jaya Maa
Devi Durge Jaya Jaya Maa
Devi Durge Jaya Jaya Maa

Kali kapalini Maa, Jagatodharini Maa
Kali kapalini Maa, Jagatodharini Maa
Devi Jaya Jaya Jaya Jaya Maa
Devi Jaya Jaya Jaya Jaya Maa

Durge Durge, Durge Jaya Jaya Maa
Durge Durge, Durge Jaya Jaya Maa

Anand rupini Maa, Karuna Sagari Maa
Anand rupini Maa, Karuna Sagari Maa
Devi Jaya Jaya Jaya Jaya Maa
Devi Jaya Jaya Jaya Jaya Maa

Durge Durge, Durge Jaya Jaya Maa
Durge Durge, Durge Jaya Jaya Maa
Devi Durge Durge, Durge Jaya Jaya Maa
Devi Durge Durge, Durge Jaya Jaya Maa

Devi Durge Jaya Jaya Maa
Devi Durge Jaya Jaya Maa
Devi Durge Jaya Jaya Maa
Devi Durge Jaya Jaya Maa

Latin Transliteration Chart

International Alphabet of Sanskrit Transliteration (I.A.S.T.)

a	ā	i	ī	u	ū	ṛ	ṝ	ḷ	
अ	आ	इ	ई	उ	ऊ	ऋ	ॠ	ऌ	
						◌ृ	◌ॄ	◌ॢ	
e	ai	o	au	ṃ	m̐	ḥ	Ardha Visarga	oṃ	
ए	ऐ	ओ	औ	◌ं	◌ँ	◌ः	◌ᳲ	ॐ	
Consonants shown with vowel 'a= अ' for uttering									
ka	क	ca	च	ṭa	ट	ta	त	pa	प
kha	ख	cha	छ	ṭha	ठ	tha	थ	pha	फ
ga	ग	ja	ज	ḍa	ड	da	द	ba	ब
gha	घ	jha	झ	ḍha	ढ	dha	ध	bha	भ
ṅa	ङ	ña	ञ	ṇa	ण	na	न	ma	म
ya	ra	la	va		ḷa	'			
य	र	ल	व		ळ	ऽ			
					Consonant only				
śa	ṣa	sa	ha		ka	क्अ = क			
श	ष	स	ह		k	क्			

Verses for Chanting

॥ अथ तन्त्रोक्तं देवी सूक्तम् ॥

नमो देव्यै महादेव्यै शिवायै सततं नमः ।
नमः प्रकृत्यै भद्रायै नियताः प्रणताः स्म ताम् ॥ १ ॥
रौद्रायै नमो नित्यायै गौर्यै धात्र्यै नमो नमः ।
ज्योत्स्नायै चेन्दुरूपिण्यै सुखायै सततं नमः ॥ २ ॥
कल्याण्यै प्रणतां वृद्ध्यै सिद्ध्यै कुर्मो नमो नमः ।
नैर्ऋत्यै भूभृतां लक्ष्म्यै शर्वाण्यै ते नमो नमः ॥ ३ ॥
दुर्गायै दुर्गपारायै सारायै सर्वकारिण्यै ।
ख्यात्यै तथैव कृष्णायै धूम्रायै सततं नमः ॥ ४ ॥
अतिसौम्यातिरौद्रायै नतास्तस्यै नमो नमः ।
नमो जगत्प्रतिष्ठायै देव्यै कृत्यै नमो नमः ॥ ५ ॥

या देवी सर्वभूतेषु विष्णुमायेति शब्दिता ।
नमस्तस्यै नमस्तस्यै नमस्तस्यै नमो नमः ॥ ६ ॥
या देवी सर्वभूतेषु चेतनेत्यभिधीयते ।
नमस्तस्यै नमस्तस्यै नमस्तस्यै नमो नमः ॥ ७ ॥
या देवी सर्वभूतेषु बुद्धिरूपेण संस्थिता ।
नमस्तस्यै नमस्तस्यै नमस्तस्यै नमो नमः ॥ ८ ॥
या देवी सर्वभूतेषु निद्रारूपेण संस्थिता ।
नमस्तस्यै नमस्तस्यै नमस्तस्यै नमो नमः ॥ ९ ॥
या देवी सर्वभूतेषु क्षुधारूपेण संस्थिता ।
नमस्तस्यै नमस्तस्यै नमस्तस्यै नमो नमः ॥ १० ॥

या देवी सर्वभूतेषु छायारूपेण संस्थिता ।
नमस्तस्यै नमस्तस्यै नमस्तस्यै नमो नमः ॥ ११ ॥
या देवी सर्वभूतेषु शक्तिरूपेण संस्थिता ।
नमस्तस्यै नमस्तस्यै नमस्तस्यै नमो नमः ॥ १२ ॥
या देवी सर्वभूतेषु तृष्णारूपेण संस्थिता ।
नमस्तस्यै नमस्तस्यै नमस्तस्यै नमो नमः ॥ १३ ॥
या देवी सर्वभूतेषु क्षान्तिरूपेण संस्थिता ।
नमस्तस्यै नमस्तस्यै नमस्तस्यै नमो नमः ॥ १४ ॥
या देवी सर्वभूतेषु जातिरूपेण संस्थिता ।
नमस्तस्यै नमस्तस्यै नमस्तस्यै नमो नमः ॥ १५ ॥
या देवी सर्वभूतेषु लज्जारूपेण संस्थिता ।
नमस्तस्यै नमस्तस्यै नमस्तस्यै नमो नमः ॥ १६ ॥
या देवी सर्वभूतेषु शान्तिरूपेण संस्थिता ।
नमस्तस्यै नमस्तस्यै नमस्तस्यै नमो नमः ॥ १७ ॥
या देवी सर्वभूतेषु श्रद्धारूपेण संस्थिता ।
नमस्तस्यै नमस्तस्यै नमस्तस्यै नमो नमः ॥ १८ ॥
या देवी सर्वभूतेषु कान्तिरूपेण संस्थिता ।
नमस्तस्यै नमस्तस्यै नमस्तस्यै नमो नमः ॥ १९ ॥
या देवी सर्वभूतेषु लक्ष्मीरूपेण संस्थिता ।
नमस्तस्यै नमस्तस्यै नमस्तस्यै नमो नमः ॥ २० ॥
या देवी सर्वभूतेषु वृत्तिरूपेण संस्थिता ।
नमस्तस्यै नमस्तस्यै नमस्तस्यै नमो नमः ॥ २१ ॥
या देवी सर्वभूतेषु स्मृतिरूपेण संस्थिता ।
नमस्तस्यै नमस्तस्यै नमस्तस्यै नमो नमः ॥ २२ ॥
या देवी सर्वभूतेषु दयारूपेण संस्थिता ।
नमस्तस्यै नमस्तस्यै नमस्तस्यै नमो नमः ॥ २३ ॥

या देवी सर्वभूतेषु तुष्टिरूपेण संस्थिता ।
नमस्तस्यै नमस्तस्यै नमस्तस्यै नमो नमः ॥ २४ ॥
या देवी सर्वभूतेषु मातृरूपेण संस्थिता ।
नमस्तस्यै नमस्तस्यै नमस्तस्यै नमो नमः ॥ २५ ॥
या देवी सर्वभूतेषु भ्रान्तिरूपेण संस्थिता ।
नमस्तस्यै नमस्तस्यै नमस्तस्यै नमो नमः ॥ २६ ॥

इन्द्रियाणामधिष्ठात्री भूतानां चाखिलेषु या ।
भूतेषु सततं तस्यै व्याप्तिदेव्यै नमो नमः ॥ २७ ॥
चितिरूपेण या कृत्स्नमेतद् व्याप्य स्थिता जगत् ।
नमस्तस्यै नमस्तस्यै नमस्तस्यै नमो नमः ॥ २८ ॥

स्तुता सुरैः पूर्वमभीष्टसंश्रयात्
तथा सुरेन्द्रेण दिनेषु सेविता ।
करोतु सा नः शुभहेतुरीश्वरी
शुभानि भद्राण्यभिहन्तु चापदः ॥ २९ ॥
या साम्प्रतं चोद्धतदैत्यतापितैः
अस्माभिरीशा च सुरैर्नमस्यते ।
या च स्मृता तत्क्षणमेव हन्ति नः
सर्वापदो भक्तिविनम्रमूर्तिभिः ॥ ३० ॥

Note: No of Verses = 5+18+3+4 = 30.

- Prayer Verses = 5
- Devi Stuti Verses = 18
- Aarti Verses = 3
- Offering Verses = 4

॥ atha tantroktaṃ devī sūktam ॥

namo devyai mahādevyai śivāyai satataṃ namaḥ ।
namaḥ prakṛtyai bhadrāyai niyatāḥ praṇatāḥ sma tām॥1
raudrāyai namo nityāyai gauryai dhātryai namo namaḥ ।
jyotsnāyai cendurūpiṇyai sukhāyai satataṃ namaḥ ॥ 2 ॥
kalyāṇyai praṇatāṃ vṛddhyai siddhyai kurmo namo namaḥ । nairṛtyai bhūbhṛtāṃ lakṣmyai śarvāṇyai te namo namaḥ ॥ 3 ॥
durgāyai durgapārāyai sārāyai sarvakāriṇyai ।
khyātyai tathaiva kṛṣṇāyai dhūmrāyai satataṃ namaḥ ॥4
atisaumyātiraudrāyai natāstasyai namo namaḥ ।
namo jagatpratiṣṭhāyai devyai kṛtyai namo namaḥ ॥ 5 ॥

yā devī sarvabhūteṣu viṣṇumāyeti śabditā ।
namastasyai namastasyai namastasyai namo namaḥ ॥ 6 ॥
yā devī sarvabhūteṣu cetanetyabhidhīyate ।
namastasyai namastasyai namastasyai namo namaḥ ॥ 7 ॥
yā devī sarvabhūteṣu buddhirūpeṇa saṃsthitā ।
namastasyai namastasyai namastasyai namo namaḥ ॥ 8 ॥
yā devī sarvabhūteṣu nidrārūpeṇa saṃsthitā ।
namastasyai namastasyai namastasyai namo namaḥ ॥ 9 ॥
yā devī sarvabhūteṣu kṣudhārūpeṇa saṃsthitā ।
namastasyai namastasyai namastasyai namo namaḥ ॥10 ॥
yā devī sarvabhūteṣu chāyārūpeṇa saṃsthitā ।
namastasyai namastasyai namastasyai namo namaḥ ॥11 ॥

yā devī sarvabhūteṣu śaktirūpeṇa saṃsthitā ।
namastasyai namastasyai namastasyai namo namaḥ ॥12
॥
yā devī sarvabhūteṣu tṛṣṇārūpeṇa saṃsthitā ।
namastasyai namastasyai namastasyai namo namaḥ ॥13
॥
yā devī sarvabhūteṣu kṣāntirūpeṇa saṃsthitā ।
namastasyai namastasyai namastasyai namo namaḥ ॥14
॥
yā devī sarvabhūteṣu jātirūpeṇa saṃsthitā ।
namastasyai namastasyai namastasyai namo namaḥ ॥15
॥
yā devī sarvabhūteṣu lajjārūpeṇa saṃsthitā ।
namastasyai namastasyai namastasyai namo namaḥ ॥16
॥
yā devī sarvabhūteṣu śāntirūpeṇa saṃsthitā ।
namastasyai namastasyai namastasyai namo namaḥ ॥17
॥
yā devī sarvabhūteṣu śraddhārūpeṇa saṃsthitā ।
namastasyai namastasyai namastasyai namo namaḥ ॥18
॥
yā devī sarvabhūteṣu kāntirūpeṇa saṃsthitā ।
namastasyai namastasyai namastasyai namo namaḥ ॥19
॥
yā devī sarvabhūteṣu lakṣmīrūpeṇa saṃsthitā ।
namastasyai namastasyai namastasyai namo namaḥ ॥20
॥
yā devī sarvabhūteṣu vṛttirūpeṇa saṃsthitā ।
namastasyai namastasyai namastasyai namo namaḥ ॥21
॥
yā devī sarvabhūteṣu smṛtirūpeṇa saṃsthitā ।
namastasyai namastasyai namastasyai namo namaḥ ॥22

yā devī sarvabhūteṣu dayārūpeṇa saṃsthitā ।
namastasyai namastasyai namastasyai namo namaḥ ॥23
॥

yā devī sarvabhūteṣu tuṣṭirūpeṇa saṃsthitā ।
namastasyai namastasyai namastasyai namo namaḥ ॥24
॥
yā devī sarvabhūteṣu mātṛrūpeṇa saṃsthitā ।
namastasyai namastasyai namastasyai namo namaḥ ॥25
॥
yā devī sarvabhūteṣu bhrāntirūpeṇa saṃsthitā ।
namastasyai namastasyai namastasyai namo namaḥ ॥26
॥

indriyāṇāmadhiṣṭhātrī bhūtānāṃ cākhileṣu yā ।
bhūteṣu satataṃ tasyai vyāptidevyai namo namaḥ ॥ 27
citirūpeṇa yā kṛtsnametad vyāpya sthitā jagat ।
namastasyai namastasyai namastasyai namo namaḥ ॥28

stutā suraiḥ pūrvamabhīṣṭasaṃśrayāt
tathā surendreṇa dineṣu sevitā ।
karotu sā naḥ śubhaheturīśvarī
śubhāni bhadrāṇyabhihantu cāpadaḥ ॥ 29 ॥
yā sāmpratam coddhatadaityatāpitaiḥ
asmābhirīśā ca surairnamasyate ।
yā ca smṛtā tatkṣaṇameva hanti naḥ
sarvāpado bhaktivinamramūrtibhiḥ ॥ 30 ॥

Sanskrit Grammar

Sandhis separated word by word पदच्छेद (प०),
and with विभक्ति Cases have been listed.

Abbreviations

Nouns

m masculine, **f** feminine, **n** neuter; **V** vocative
1/1 = vibhakti from 1 to 7/number 1 to 3
adj = adjective, adv = adverb

Indeclinables (uninflected nouns or verbs) **0.**
In Sanskrit the **adverbs** are mostly uninflected.
Adjective follows a Substantive in case and number.

Verbs

iii/1 = person i to iii / number 1 to 3
PPP = Past Participle Passive = क्त
PPA = Past Participle Active = क्तवत्
PrPA = Present Participle Active = शतृ / शानच्
FPA = Future Participle Active = लृट् + शतृ
PoPP = Potential Participle Passive = य, तव्य,
अनीयर् (gerundive)

It is a common practice in Sanskrit grammar to use a "hyphen" to indicate compounds.
Compound or समास is frequently encountered in Sanskrit literature. It has a beauty and a brevity.

Since Sanskrit is an inflectional language, the **spelling of the same word** changes as per context or usage. Hence words can be **placed anywhere** in a sentence, as in poetic use, without change in meaning. The matrix shows how.

Verb inflections in Sanskrit – a sample chart

982 गम्लृ गतौ – to go, also in the sense of attainment			
Present Tense Active voice लट् कर्त्तरि			
Person/no	singular	dual	plural
Third	गच्छति [iii/1]	गच्छतः [iii/2]	गच्छन्ति [iii/3]
Second	गच्छसि [ii/1]	गच्छथः [ii/2]	गच्छथ [ii/3]
First	गच्छामि [i/1]	गच्छावः [i/2]	गच्छामः [i/3]

Noun declensions in Sanskrit – a sample chart

Masculine stem, vowel अ ending			
(र्–आ–म्–अ) राम [m] Lord’s name			
	singular [1]	dual [2]	plural [3]
1 Doer	रामः [1/1]	रामौ [1/2]	रामाः [1/3]
2 Object	रामम् [2/1]	रामौ [2/2]	रामान् [2/3]
3 by	रामेण [3/1]	रामाभ्याम् [3/2]	रामैः [3/3]
4 for	रामाय [4/1]	रामाभ्याम् [4/2]	रामेभ्यः [4/3]
5 from	रामात् [5/1]	रामाभ्याम् [5/2]	रामेभ्यः [5/3]
6 of	रामस्य [6/1]	रामयोः [6/2]	रामाणाम् [6/3]
7 in	रामे [7/1]	रामयोः [7/2]	रामेषु [7/3]
Vocative	हे राम [V/1]	हे रामौ [V/2]	हे रामाः [V/3]

Masculine stem, consonant त् ending

मरुत् m Wind, Breeze, Air			
	singular 1	dual 2	plural 3
1 Doer	मरुत् 1/1	मरुतौ 1/2	मरुतः 1/3
2 Object	मरुतम् 2/1	मरुतौ 2/2	मरुतः 2/3
3 by	मरुता 3/1	मरुद्भ्याम् 3/2	मरुद्भिः 3/3
4 for	मरुते 4/1	मरुद्भ्याम् 4/2	मरुद्भ्यः 4/3
5 from	मरुतः 5/1	मरुद्भ्याम् 5/2	मरुद्भ्यः 5/3
6 of	मरुतः 6/1	मरुतोः 6/2	मरुताम् 6/3
7 in	मरुति 7/1	मरुतोः 7/2	मरुत्सु 7/3
Vocative	हे मरुत् V/1	हे मरुतौ V/2	हे मरुतः V/3

Moods and Tenses in Sanskrit

1	लट्	Present Tense
2	लुङ्	Aorist Past Tense,before from now
3	लङ्	Imperfect Past Tense – before from yesterday onwards
4	लिट्	Perfect Past Tense – distant unseen past
5	लृट्	Simple Future Tense – now onwards
6	लुट्	Periphrastic Future Tense – tomorrow onwards
7	लृङ्	Conditional Mood - if/then, past or future
8	लोट्	Imperative Mood – request
9	विधि॰	Potential Mood – order विधिलिङ्
10	आशीर्	Benedictive Mood – blessing आशीर्लिङ् (also used in the sense of a curse)

Conjugation process of Verb

अभिधीयते लट् iii/1 = she supports, preserves, upholds

Root 1136 √ धीङ् आधारे आदाने अनादरे च । 4cA

1.3.1 भूवादयो धातवः । धीङ्

1.3.3 हलन्त्यम् । 1.3.9 तस्य लोपः । धी

3.4.69 लः कर्मणि च भावे चाकर्मकेभ्यः । धी

3.2.123 वर्तमाने लट् । 3.4.77 लस्य । धी + लँट्

1.3.3 हलन्त्यम् । 1.3.9 तस्य लोपः । धी + लँ

1.3.2 उपदेशेऽजनुनासिक इत् । 1.3.9 तस्य लोपः । धी + ल्

3.4.78 तिप्तस्झिसिप्थस्थमिब्वस्मस् तातांझथासाथांध्वमिड्वहिमहिङ् ।

Atmanepada धी + तातांझ । conjugating third person

1.4.101 तिङस्त्रीणि त्रीणि प्रथममध्यमोत्तमाः ।

1.4.102 तान्येकवचनद्विवचनबहुवचनान्येकशः । धी + त । singular

1.4.108 शेषे प्रथमः । known as Prathma Purusha

3.4.113 तिङ्शित्सार्वधातुकम् । धी + त

3.1.68 कर्तरि शप् । 3.1.69 दिवादिभ्यः श्यन् । धी + श्यन् + त

1.3.8 लशक्वतद्धिते । 1.3.3 हलन्त्यम् । 1.3.9 तस्य लोपः ।

धी + य + त ।

3.4.79 टित आत्मनेपदानां टेरे । धी + य + ते ।

1.2.4 सार्वधातुकमपित् । धी + य + ते ।

= धीयते लट् iii/1 । She supports.

With Upasarga अभि + धीयते = अभिधीयते लट् iii/1 ।

She fully supports. She preserves well. She tightly holds. The Mother cares for deeply.

Declension process of Noun

देवी = Goddess, Glow of Light, Sweet and Bright

Stem देवी f → देवी f 1/1

1.2.45 अर्थवदधातुरप्रत्ययः प्रातिपदिकम् । देवी

1.2.46 कृत्तद्धितसमासाश्च । 3.1.1 प्रत्ययः । 3.1.2 परश्च ।

4.1.1 ङ्याप्प्रातिपदिकात्

4.1.2 स्वौजस-

मौट्छष्टाभ्याम्भिस्ङेभ्याम्भ्यस्ङसिभ्याम्भ्यस्ङसोसाम्ङ्योस्सुप् ।

1.4.104 विभक्तिश्च । 1.4.103 सुपः = use one of these vibhakti suffix. देवी + सुँ ।

1.4.22 द्व्येकयोर्द्विवचनैकवचने = singular number taken.

देवी + सुँ 1/1 ।

1.3.2 उपदेशेऽजनुनासिक इत् । 1.3.9 तस्य लोपः । देवी + स् ।

6.1.68 हल्ङ्याब्भ्यो दीर्घात् सुतिस्यपृक्तं हल् । देवी ।

= देवी f1/1 । *Feminine. First case singular.*

Goddess. Attractive Light. Delightful form.
Evoking Sweetness. Giving Protection.

References

https://www.ashtangayoga.info/philosophy/sanskrit-and-devanagari/transliteration-tool/
https://ashtadhyayi.com/
https://sanskrit.uohyd.ac.in/scl/
https://www.sanskritworld.in/sanskrittool/SanskritVerb/tiGanta.html
Ya Devi Sarva Bhuteshu by Dr Manikantan
https://www.youtube.com/watch?v=ynWceZ7Jfe8
Ya Devi (Deep Relaxation)
https://www.youtube.com/watch?v=B-zKpBLILs8
Devi Suktam with Sanskrit Lyrics
https://www.youtube.com/watch?v=Kw0neisiXk4
Devi Suktam by Alka Yagnik
https://www.youtube.com/watch?v=dhE1JFVfBUQ

https://www.vyasaonline.com/markandeya-purana/
https://www.gitapress.org/bookdetail/sankshipta-markandeya-puran-hindi-539
https://www.exoticindiaart.com/book/details/markandeya-purana-khemraj-edition-nza358/

Ram Narayan Duttji Shastri – श्री दुर्गा सप्तशती (विशिष्ट संस्करण) 1281 – 1st, 73rd reprint – 2020 – Gita Press.

Rishi Kumar Shastri – श्री दुर्गा सप्तशती भाषा – 1st – 1990 – Kamal Pustakalaya, Nai Sarak, Delhi.

Ashwini Kumar Aggarwal
– Dhatupatha of Panini – 2nd – 2017 –
– Sanskrit Grammar Playful Enquiry – 1st – 2020 –
– Sanskrit Noun Declension using Ashtadhyayi Sutras – 1st – 2022 – Devotees of Sri Sri Ravi Shankar Ashram.

Epilogue

Sing freely.
Sing from your Soul.
Sing whenever you want.

Offer all to Her and rest deeply.

सर्वे भवन्तु सुखिनः । सर्वे सन्तु निरामयाः ।
सर्वे भद्राणि पश्यन्तु । मा कश्चिद् दुःख भाग् भवेत् ॥
ॐ शान्तिः शान्तिः शान्तिः ॥

When faith has blossomed in life,
Every step is led by the Divine.

Sri Sri Ravi Shankar

Om Namah Shivaya

जय गुरुदेव

www.ingramcontent.com/pod-product-compliance
Lightning Source LLC
Chambersburg PA
CBHW050024170726
48282CB00025B/531
* 9 7 8 9 3 9 5 7 6 6 5 1 7 *